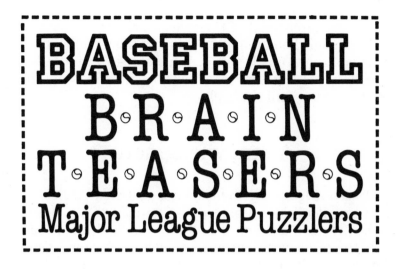

BASEBALL
B·R·A·I·N
T·E·A·S·E·R·S
Major League Puzzlers

Dom Forker

- - - - -

Drawings by Sandy Hoffman

Sterling Publishing Co., Inc.   New York

Dedication

To Ted, Son-Number-Three, who celebrated his 16th birthday on the day that I celebrated the completion of this book—we finally did it. You were last in order, but certainly not least in rank. Next time around, you'll be first in order, with the book.

Acknowledgment

I acknowledge my indebtedness to David A. Boehm, Sterling Publishing Company's Chairman of the Board, who provided me with the idea for *Baseball Brain Teasers*. His enthusiastic encouragement and active assistance in the search for the best possible "brain teasers" have been indispensable to the creation, the development, and the completion of this book.

Library of Congress Cataloging-in-Publication Data
Forker, Dom.
  Baseball brain teasers.
  Includes index.
  1. Baseball—Rules. I. Title.
GV877.F59 1986   796.357′02′022   85-27955
ISBN 0-8069-6282-8
ISBN 0-8069-6284-4 (pbk.)
ISBN 0-8069-6283-6 (lib. bdg.)

CONTENTS

(continued)

Introduction

The purpose of this book is threefold: 1) to inform, 2) to entertain, and 3) to intrigue.

Baseball, on the surface, is a very simple game. Beneath the surface, however, it is a very complex sport. The National Pastime has been played for 86 years—since 1900—in the modern era. Every play that has ever taken place on a major league diamond is covered in the rule book and its amendments. The umpires know the official rule book from cover to cover. Yet, new and unusual plays are constantly taking place, before they can be covered in the rule book, and umpires are still huddling with each other to interpret these new situations. If the official interpreters of the game can be stumped, it is not surprising that we, fans, reporters and followers of the sport, can be confused, too.

Some of the new twists that have come up include the following: 1) a team getting four outs in one inning, 2) a batter hitting the ball fair three times in one official at-bat, 3) a runner stealing first base, and 4) a batter-runner circling the bases in reverse order after a home run!

Would you anticipate such plays? Of course not. Does the umpire anticipate such plays? Again, the answer is no. But he has to be ready to react to them. He has to be *informed*. So should you. This book will teach you to be in the right position to call these tricky plays.

Baseball, on the surface, is a very structured sport. Beneath the surface, however, as sports announcer Joe Garagiola has said, it can be a *funny* game. You will find some humorous incidents in these pages.

Baseball, on the surface, is pretty routine. Beneath the surface, however, it can be very dramatic. A baseball game, like a good short story, often ends dramatically at the high point of the action. That adds intrigue.

Intriguing situations. This book is full of them. But, hopefully, the next time that those around you don't know the baseball rule, you will!

Is he out or is he safe? Which umpire do you believe?
(courtesy of Los Angeles Dodgers)

☉ 1 ☉

IS THAT ALL THERE IS
TO BASE RUNNING?

Who's on Third?

The Yankees are at bat with one out and the bases loaded. Boston's pitcher hurls a fast ball right down the center of the plate, and the batter rockets it off the left-center-field fence. The ball bounces back towards the left fielder.

The runner at third scores easily. The runner at second takes a wide turn at third, hesitates, and, for some reason, returns to the bag. The runner at first sees the traffic jam at third and slides into the base. The batter, who has been running hard all the way, but with his head down, races into third with a stand-up "triple."

The Red Sox third baseman is confused, too, when he gets the throw from the left fielder. He knows that two of the runners don't belong there. But he doesn't know which two. So he does the obvious: he tags all three runners. The umpire calls two of them out. But which two? Who, do you think, has the right to be there?

*   *   *

Since there was no force play in effect, the runner from

Three's a crowd.

second has sole right to the base as he arrived there first. The other two are trespassers, and are out.

* * *

Babe Herman of the 1926 Dodgers "tripled" into a double play under similar circumstances. Herman, who, in his younger years, ran the bases like a runaway stagecoach, became much too cautious after that double-play incident, however. Teammates were constantly complaining about him, because they were passing the hesitant Herman on the base paths. He never wanted to end up on the same base with a teammate again!

Since that day, whenever someone says, "The Dodgers have three men on base," a listener with a keen sense of humor will comically say, "Which base?"

Second Comes First

When with the Oakland A's, Rickey Henderson is on first base in a game against the White Sox.

On the first pitch to the next batter, Rickey takes off for second. The batter swings and hits a fly ball down the left-field line. Henderson runs and dives head first into second. From his prone position Rickey sees that the left fielder has a good chance to catch the ball; so he scurries to his feet and hurries back to first. But the ball eludes the left-fielder's outstretched glove and bounces into the left-field stands for a ground-rule double.

Henderson, who is embarrassed, knows that the ball is dead; so he takes a shortcut across the infield: from first to third.

Is he allowed to do this?

* * *

Henderson, who *knows* that he can't miss a base, should not have used the shortcut route. The umpires weren't caught off-guard, though. They knew that a player, in order to get to third, had to touch second first. When the White Sox appealed the play and threw the ball to second, the base he failed to touch, the umpires called Rickey out.

Third base became a souvenir.

You Can't Touch 'em All

A player who is not noted for long-ball slugging surprises himself and everyone in the ballpark by hitting a fence-clearing blast.

When he trots around the bases, however, he misses touching both third and home plate.

Is his hit still a home run? If not, what kind of a hit is he awarded?

*   *   *

If the opponents, noticing the errors of commission, call for an appeal play, the hit does not stand as a home run. If the appeal is made at home, the batter-runner gets a triple; if the appeal is at third, he gets a double.

* * *

In the American League playoffs of 1976, Chris Chambliss of the Yankees did that exact thing; but he got credit for a pennant-winning homer, even though all of the umpires and the Royal players knew that he had missed third base and home.

When Chambliss cleared the fence with his four-base blast in the home half of the ninth, the sellout crowd poured onto the field in droves. Third base was carried away as a souvenir. Home plate was dug up for the same reason. So Chambliss stepped where he thought third base and home plate once were.

Manager Billy Martin even insisted that Chambliss leave the clubhouse and once again step on the spot from which home plate had been removed.

There was nothing to worry about, though. When the umpires saw the screaming crowd streaming onto the field, they decided under the circumstances that Chambliss had touched all the bases, and they bolted towards their locker room for safety.

Who Says You Can't Steal First?

Let's suppose the Cardinals have runners on third and first, with two out, in the bottom of the ninth inning of a tie game with the Braves.

The Cardinals' slugger is at the plate. The runner on first, anxious to have his team score the winning run, takes off for second with the pitcher's first offering to the batter, hoping to draw a throw that will let his teammate score from third. The Braves' catcher holds on to the ball, however; and the Cardinals now have runners on second and third with two out.

On the following pitch, the runner on second surprises everyone at Busch Stadium in St. Louis: he attempts to *steal* first base! The catcher, who has been taken off-guard, throws late to first while the runner on third scores the winning run before the Braves' first baseman can make the return throw to the catcher. However, the home plate umpire has his arms in the air signaling "time out."

Does anyone get a stolen base and do the Cardinals "steal" the winning run?

*   *   *

The answer to both questions is "no." The runner "stealing" first is called out for making a travesty of the game, by running the bases in reverse order. And the umpire's time out, which preceded the play at home, creates a dead-ball situation. No runner can advance.

*   *   *

Germany Schaefer of Detroit actually did steal first base in a game between the Tigers and the Indians, about 1908. Nig Clarke of Cleveland was the catcher and he held on to the ball. But on the next pitch, when Schaefer set off for second again, the embarrassed catcher threw the ball into

Point of no return—first base.

center field; and Davy Jones scored the winning run from third.

At that time there was no rule preventing a runner from stealing a base in reverse order. The next day the rules were changed, however; and now the umpires have one less problem to worry about: for no one has been able to steal first base again!

Touching Base

Ron Kittle of the White Sox is supposed to be a playful player.

Let's say that one day Kittle hits a pitch over the roof at Comiskey Park for his 100th major league home run. Wishing to cherish the moment, Kittle runs the bases in reverse instead of forward. He runs from home to third, to second, to first, and back to home.

Will Kittle's blow be officially recorded as a home run?

*   *   *

No, Kittle would be called out for running the bases in reverse, thereby making a travesty, or farce, of the game.

*   *   *

Did this ever happen? It sure did.

Jimmy Piersall of the 1963 Mets did just that. On the day he hit his 100th major league home run, he ran the bases in reverse order. There was no rule in effect at that time that prohibited a runner from doing so. There is now.

On the day after Piersall took his zany route, the rule book was amended to read that on a home run each advance base has to be touched in order. So Kittle can't legally do it, even if he would like to.

The Runner Who Balked

In the top of the fifth inning, the pitcher is called for a balk, but he continues his delivery to the batter. The runner on first, when he hears the balk call, starts trotting to second. However, when the batter hits a long fly ball to the fence, which is caught by the center fielder, the runner becomes confused. Afraid that he is going to be doubled off first, he retreats to the base from which he came.

The first baseman tags the runner when he returns to first base and claims he is out because he should be on second.

Is the runner out?

*   *   *

No, he is not out. The balk takes precedence over the action that follows. Because it does, the runner gets a one-base advance, and the batter gets to hit again.

*   *   *

The balk becomes a sensitive issue when the pitcher delivers the ball and the batter hits it. That was the case in a Montreal-San Francisco game.

The Expo pitcher threw the ball after the umpire had made the balk call, and the Giants' Jack Clark flew out to the fence. The base runner didn't know what to do. He heard the umpire call "balk" and he saw the ball being hit. At first, he ran. However, when he saw the ball being relayed to first, he retreated.

Though he didn't know why at the time, he had two reasons why he shouldn't have been concerned about being put out: 1) the balk took precedence over the hit, and 2) the balk created a dead-ball situation.

A runner can't be put out when the ball isn't in play.

The takeout slide.

Takeout for Two

Suppose the Blue Jays have runners on first and second with one out in the bottom of the ninth. The Brewers lead by one run.

The Blue Jays' batter hits a one-hopper to the third baseman, who throws to second for one out. The Brewer second baseman pivots for the throw to first; but the Blue Jay runner slides hard at the fielder, instead of the base, taking the second baseman out of the play.

Does the umpire punish the offensive team?

* * *

The umpire, if he is interpreting the play according to the rule book, should call the batter-runner out at first base, creating a double play and giving the Brewers a one-run win. (The thinking is that the illegal slide prevented the pivot man from turning the double play.) But unfortunately the umpires don't call this play consistently. The situation listed below is an example.

* * *

In a key play in the 1976 playoffs, between the Royals and the Yankees, Hal McRae in sliding into second took Willie Randolph out of the play in such a fashion. The umpire let the play stand. Such plays usually lead to get-even-type baseball.

The next time, however, the umpire might call the batter-runner out.

The Bounce Slide

In the top of the tenth inning in a tight game, a runner races home on a single and slides without a play being made on him.

The catcher, receiving the late throw, notices that the umpire does not make a call. He rushes after the runner, who is walking to the dugout, and tags him.

Why, in this case, does the umpire not make a call? Is the runner safe or out?

* * *

No call by the umpire indicates that the runner is neither safe nor out. On this play, the runner misses touching home plate, so he isn't safe. But since he wasn't tagged initially, he isn't out, either. When the catcher runs after him and tags him, then the runner is out.

* * *

When Gil Hodges was managing the Washington Senators, he was victimized by such a play. One of his players slid "across" the plate without a play being made. When the Oriole catcher realized that a call hadn't been made, he tagged the surprised runner out.

Hodges angrily faced the umpire and demanded to know how his runner could be out when a play hadn't been made on him. The umpire informed Hodges that when the Senator runner slid, he *bounced* over the plate.

The bounce slide.

The Shortest Distance

In a game in Minnesota, the Twins' Rod Carew, an excellent base runner, is on first with one out. The next batter hits what appears to be a certain extra-base hit to left-center field. At least Carew thinks so, for he is rounding second, digging for third.

But Freddie Lynn, the Boston center fielder, makes a sensational diving catch, causing Gene Mauch, the third-base coach, to throw up his hands and to yell at Carew, "Go back to first!" Rod applies the brakes and returns to first by the shortest distance: from third to first. Second baseman Rick Burleson, seeing Carew taking a shortcut to first, hurries his relay throw and misfires, the ball going into the Boston dugout.

Is Carew out for failing to retouch second base, or is he awarded third for the two-base penalty that that dead-ball overthrow warrants?

* * *

In this comedy-of-errors scene, the second error has no bearing on the original one. Until the Red Sox appeal Carew's missing second, however, the umpire has to place the runner on third because of the two-base overthrow. But, upon proper appeal, the umpire will call Carew out for failing to retouch second base.

The umpire, after the relay throw ended up in the dugout, said to Carew, "You, third base!" But, after the proper appeal, he said, "You, out!"

Tail-End Play

Garry Templeton is on second and Gene Tenace is on first as the Cardinals bat in the top of the sixth inning in a game at Philadelphia.

On Steve Carlton's first pitch to the next batter, Templeton takes off for third, and Tenace breaks for second. Catcher Bob Boone, sensing that he has no chance to throw out the speedy Templeton at third, throws to second, hoping to catch the slow-footed Tenace. Second baseman Manny Trillo applies the tag in plenty of time for the inning-ending out.

Does Templeton, who did not draw a throw, get credit for a steal on an inning-ending out?

*   *   *

No, he does not get credit for a stolen base. When a double or a triple steal is attempted and one runner is thrown out before reaching and holding the base he is attempting to steal, no other runner is credited with a stolen base.

"Did he catch it?"

Runner in Reverse

With a teammate on first base, the batter hits a pop fly that both the second baseman and right fielder misplay.

It ultimately falls to the ground for an apparent hit. The runner on first, thinking that the right fielder is going to catch the ball, runs back to first base. The batter, seeing the ball drop safely, rounds first and then retreats to the bag. In rounding first, however, he passes his teammate, who was returning to the base.

Now there are two runners on first. The first baseman, who takes the throw from the outfield, tags both runners.

Which one is out?

* * *

The runner who was first is legally on first. When he passed his teammate, the batter-runner was officially called out. Had the batter-runner not passed his teammate, the runner from first would have been the out at second, because a force play would have been in effect; and the batter would have been the legal runner at first.

*   *   *

The 1985 Cubs, following the above script, had runners passing each other in opposite directions. Ryne Sandberg of the Cubs hit a fly ball that the Dodgers' Steve Sax and Mike Marshall misplayed. Marshall finally lost the ball in the sun. Sandberg then proceeded to pass runner Bob Dernier, who was hustling back to first. Seeing Marshall retrieve the ball, Sandberg returned to first, which was already occupied by Dernier.

The umpires lost the ball in the "sun," too. They called the wrong runner—Dernier—out on the play.

The Runner's Route

The best base runner of the Cardinals takes a big lead against the crafty veteran southpaw for the Phillies.

The pitcher, catching the runner leaning towards second, throws the ball to the first baseman, who starts the rundown of the St. Louis speedster. The first baseman tosses the ball to the second baseman, who tries to make the tag. But the runner, who squirms at least six feet out of the base path, eludes the second baseman's tag and beats his throw to the shortstop. The Phillies claim that the runner should be out, because he has run out of the base path.

Are they right?

*   *   *

Yes, the runner *should* be out.

The runner's route extends three feet to both the outfield and the infield side of the base path. The runner exceeded that distance, so he is out.

*   *   *

Some years ago, in a game at Cincinnati, Joe Morgan got called out on such a play. Morgan claimed that no umpire had ever called him out on that play before. He stressed that the rule was one which was rarely enforced.

Maybe so. But the umpire did make the right call, according to the rule book.

"Where's the base path?"

Who Blew the Cover?

In a game between the visiting Dodgers and Padres, the batter lifts a pop-up to short center field. The outfielder comes in for the ball, while the shortstop and second baseman go out for the short fly. But the ball falls untouched on the outfield grass.

The batter rounds first base and, seeing that no Padre player is covering the pivot base, continues to second, stretching a single into a double.

Whose responsibility was it to cover second base on that play?

* * *

The *first* baseman blew the cover. There was no play at first, so he could have vacated his base. If he had made the proper play, the batter would have rounded first and returned to the bag. Then if he should stray too far from first, the Dodger pitcher would be at the base for a possible play behind the runner.

* * *

In such a play, late in 1984, first baseman Leon Durham of the Cubs forgot to cover second, thus turning a single into a double.

It bears out the point that you always have to be thinking on the baseball diamond.

Hit Behind a Fielder

Suppose the Cubs have the bases loaded with one out in the top of the ninth. The Cardinals, down by one run, bring their infield in.

The batter hits a hard grounder to the right of the shortstop. The ball goes past his outstretched glove and hits the runner from second, who is behind the shortstop. The ball caroms off his knee and rolls down the left-field line into foul territory. Three runners score and the batter ends up on second.

Do the runs count?

*   *   *

Yes, the runs do count. When the runner *behind* the fielder gets struck with a batted ball, the ball is live and in play if, in the umpire's judgment, no other fielder had a chance to make a play on the ball. In this case, the runs score and the batter is allowed to stay at second.

*   *   *

The Reds, in a game against the Pirates, had a similar situation. They had Johnny Bench on third, George Foster on second, and Dave Concepcion on first. The score was tied in the seventh inning.

Ray Knight hit a ball past the drawn-in Tim Foli that struck Foster and kept on rolling. In the meantime, the Red runners kept on running. Legally.

Missing the Bag

Batting with two out and the bases loaded, a slugger for the Rangers hits an apparent triple; but, on an appeal play, he is called out for missing first base.

What kind of hit does he get and how many RBIs does he receive?

*   *   *

The answer to both questions is "none." When the batter, after making a safe hit, is called out for having failed to touch a base, the last base he reached safely determines the credit he gets. The batter in this case missed the first bag, so he didn't reach any base safely. He is charged with a time at bat, but no hit. Also, because he made the third out at first base, he doesn't get credited with an RBI. And the runs don't count.

*   *   *

One time, during the early days of the Mets, Marv Throneberry hit what appeared to be a certain triple; but the opposing first baseman appealed, contending that "Marvelous Marv" had missed the bag in rounding first. The appeal was upheld.

Manager Casey Stengel ran out of the dugout to argue the umpire's call, but he was stopped in his tracks by his first-base coach, who said, "Don't bother, Casey, he missed second, too."

⊖ 2 ⊖

OFF THE FENCE

Inside-the-Park Homer

A batter hits a line drive that bounces out of the glove of the left fielder and flies over the fence. The umpire rules the hit a double.

Is he right?

* * *

The umpire, in this case, is wrong and should be overruled. When an umpire miscalls a book rule, another arbiter may reverse his call. This hit should be declared a home run. In the next example, one umpire actually did overrule another one.

* * *

In a 1953 game between the Cardinals and the host Braves, Milwaukee's Bill Bruton hit a fly ball that deflected off left-fielder Enos Slaughter's glove and bounced over the fence. One umpire called the hit a double; another arbiter reversed the call and awarded the batter a home run.

The second umpire's decision, based upon the rule that a fair fly ball "in flight" that is deflected by a fielder into the stands in fair territory is a home run, was the correct one. Bruton was awarded a game-winning home run.

Is it "bounding" or "in flight?"

A Heads-Up Play

A batter hits a long fly ball that bounces off the center-field fence, strikes the outfielder on the head, and bounces into the stands. The umpire awards the batter a ground-rule double.

Is the ruling a good one?

* * *

The umpire is right when he rules that a "bounding" fair ball that is deflected by a player into the stands in fair territory is a double. Once a fly ball hits the fence, it is considered to be a "bounding" ball, not a ball "in flight," and cannot be ruled a home run. A ball "in flight"—that is, a fair fly ball that is deflected by a player into the stands in fair territory—is a home run.

* * *

The Expos' Andre Dawson, in a 1977 game at Montreal's Olympic Stadium, rocketed a long fly ball to center field that bounded off the wall, struck Dodger outfielder Rick Monday on the head, and bounced into the stands.

Dawson got a double, Monday a headache.

Eight Men on the Field

Marty Barrett of the Red Sox hits very few home runs. Understandably, he was very upset when the Yankees' Ken Griffey dived into the left-field stands at Yankee Stadium to rob the Boston second-sacker of a four-base blast.

Can an outfielder leave the playing field to make a catch?

*   *   *

Yes, an outfielder, or any other player, can leave the playing field to make a catch. The determining factor is whether the fielder's momentum carries him into the stands while he is making the play. If it does, it is a good catch. If the player establishes a stationary position in the stands before he makes the catch, however, the grab is disallowed.

*   *   *

In the situation described above, Griffey timed his jump perfectly and made a sensational catch while bouncing off a fan who was trying to snatch the ball from him. It was a legitimate catch.

If Griffey had mistimed his jump, landed in the stands early, and then caught Barrett's drive, the hit would have been ruled a home run.

But Griffey played the ball perfectly. Only his landing, back on the playing field, was a little less than smooth. Dave Winfield, playing the part of an Olympic judge, gave Griffey a ten on his dive, but only a five on his landing.

"... and then there were eight."

The Silent Speaker

In a game at the Astrodome, Mike Schmidt of the Phillies is up with runners on first and second. He hits a tremendous blast that hits the bottom side of a loudspeaker that is suspended 117 feet in the air in center field, 329 feet from home plate.

What does the umpire call?

*   *   *

The Astros do not have a ground rule, or an air rule, for that situation. The ball is "in play." The runners must advance at least one base because of the force play that is in effect. Beyond that, they advance at their own risk.

When Mike Schmidt hit that "tape-measure" blast at the Astrodome with Dave Cash and Larry Bowa on base, the ball bounced straight down and center fielder Cesar Cedeño fielded the ball on a bounce.

Schmidt got credited only with a long single! And the runners each moved up only one base.

Umpire's Judgment

Suppose a batter, with a man on first base, rips a ball that deflects off the third baseman's shin and bounces, in foul territory, down the left-field line. Then a fan reaches over the rail and touches the ball. In the meantime, the runner scores and the batter ends up on second.

Does the runner have to return to third because of the ground-rule double?

* * *

No, he does not have to return to third. The umpire rules that the runner from first could have scored whether the fan interfered with the ball, or not. The umpire has the right to grant certain awards during an interference play of this sort. In this case, the batter would have to stay at second; but the runner would be allowed to score.

* * *

This play occurred in an opening-day game between the Phillies and the Reds at Crosley Field. Richie Ashburn was the Phillie runner at first; Granny Hamner, the batter. Hamner smashed a ball off third baseman Don Hoak's shin.

The Phils of those days were known as the Whiz Kids. On that play, Ashburn "whizzed" around the bases. He scored easily as Hamner coasted into second. The Red manager argued the call, but unsuccessfully.

"Keep your filthy hands off!"

Fan Interference

The catcher in chasing a foul pop fly brakes to a halt near the dugout seats. A fan clearly leans over the rail, onto the field, and interferes with the flight of the ball. The catcher fails to make the catch.

Does the batter get another chance?

*   *   *

The batter does *not* get another chance to hit when a fan interferes with a player attempting to make a catch on the playing field. If the player is leaning across the rail into the stands, the *fan* has a right to the ball. In the case illustrated here, however, the batter is out.

*   *   *

Del Rice of the Braves had that happen to him in a game in Philadelphia. The umpire called the batter out because Rice was standing and reaching for the ball on the playing field, and he could have caught it if the fan had not interfered.

Pick-off or Pick-up?

With the bases loaded, the hurler, instead of pitching to the plate, tries to pick off the runner on first base. But the ball sails wildly into the first-base seats.

How far can the runners advance?

*   *   *

Each runner can advance one base. The rule is one base if the pitcher was on the rubber. If he had stepped off the rubber and had thrown the ball into the stands, he would have been penalized two bases per runner. If he had taken a return throw from the catcher, in front of the rubber, and hurled the ball into the first-base stands, he also would have been penalized two bases per runner.

*   *   *

Chuck Stobbs of the 1956 Senators found himself in such a situation. Pitching to the Tigers' Bob Kennedy, with his pivot foot on the rubber, he "picked off" a fan in the first-base boxes.

Each runner "picked up" a base on the play.

The Ground-Rule Triple

There are many ways in which a batter can hit a ground-rule double: 1) he can hit a ball in fair territory that bounces into the stands, 2) he can hit a ball that a fan touches in leaning over the rail, 3) he can hit a ball that deflects off any base into the stands, or 4) he can hit a ball which deflects off a fielder's glove, in fair territory, and bounces into the stands in foul territory.

By way of contrast, is there any way in which a batter can hit a ground-rule triple?

*   *   *

Baseball doesn't have a ground-rule triple today, but it once did. In the 1903 World Series, between Pittsburgh and Boston, the Pirates, because of overflow crowds, permitted fans to stand behind a rope in the outfield. Both teams agreed that any batted balls that rolled under the rope would be called ground-rule triples.

In the four games played at Pittsburgh, the Red Sox collected 12 of the 17 ground-rule triples. Tommy Leach of the Pirates hit a record four three-base hits in one World Series.

☺ 3 ☺

TRICKY TACTICS

The Player-Pitcher Switch

Let's say that the starting southpaw of the Phillies is in trouble late in a game against the Braves. Atlanta has runners on first and second, one out, and their clean-up hitter, a right-handed batter, at the plate.

The Phillies manager decides to relieve his star lefty with his best bullpen hurler, a righty. But he does not remove his star pitcher from the game. He puts him at first base and moves his first sacker to play third base. The relief pitcher gets the batter to hit a short fly ball to left field for an out. There is no advance. Then the manager returns the fielder from third to first and restores his star to the mound, to pitch to the next batter, who is a left-hand hitter.

Can a manager switch pitchers this way?

* * *

As long as he stays in the game, a pitcher can return to the mound. The pitcher who replaced him, however, has to have hurled to at least one official batter.

* * *

Manager Paul Richards of the White Sox used to be noted for that switch. One day he substituted left-hander

Billy Pierce for right-hander Harry Dorish when south-paw-swinging Ted Williams was at the plate. Richards kept Dorish in thé game, placing him at third base. When Pierce retired Williams, Dorish returned to the mound, retiring Pierce. The displaced third baseman, however, could not come back into the game.

Sometimes Richards used to keep Pierce, a good-hitting pitcher, in the game, too. Richards would put his pitcher at first base. When the situation was right, he would return his good-hitting pitcher to the mound.

The Sidewinder

The pitcher is in the stretch position. With his foot on the side of the rubber, he pitches to the batter.

Is there anything wrong with this?

* * *

The pitcher has just committed a balk. According to the rule book, the "set position" is indicated by the pitcher when he stands facing the batter with his entire foot on, or in front of, and in contact with and not off the end of the pitcher's plate, and his other foot in front of the pitcher's plate, holding the ball in both hands in front of his body and coming to a complete stop. The key wording here is "not off the end of the pitcher's plate."

* * *

Steve Blass of the winning Pirates was charged with this type of balk in the 1979 World Series. The umpire thought he was doing it too frequently, but he was the recipient of a tough call in World Series play.

Hitting for the Cycle

Baseball players are superstitious. Take the case of Hall-of-Famer Paul Waner of the Pirates.

Normally the number-three hitter in the lineup, he was switched to the number-two spot on this particular day. Caught off-guard, he was still sitting in the dugout when he should have been up at the plate. So he grabbed the first bat he could find and delivered a base hit. Then he used that procedure of selecting a bat for the rest of the game.

The results of his experiment are as follows: six at-bats, six different bats, six pitches, six hits.

The next day, however, the system does not work; so Waner returns, after the game, to his regular bat.

Should he have stayed with his experiment?

*   *   *

He might have continued with his experiment a little longer. There have been only two players, Jim Bottomley of the Cardinals in 1924 and 1931, and Roger "Doc" Cramer of the old Athletics in 1932 and 1935, who have gotten six hits in six at-bats twice during their major league careers.

Waner did it once. Who knows, though? He might have done it more times had he only had more faith in a silly superstition.

"Look where you're going!"

Who Is That Masked Man?

The teams are tied, 3–3, in the bottom half of the 12th inning.

The Giant pitcher, who is in a groove, is mowing down batter after batter. He continues until he gets to the potential second out. The batter lifts a foul fly behind the plate. The Giant catcher quickly discards his mask and circles under the ball. But he steps into his upturned mask and tumbles to the ground as the ball falls to earth untouched.

The catcher has made a physical mistake on the play. But he has committed a mental error, too. What was the mental mistake?

*   *   *

On a foul pop the catcher should never relieve himself of his mask until he knows the direction of the ball. Then he should flip the mask in the opposite direction.

*　*　*

Such a mistake cost the Giants the 1924 World Series. With the seventh game, against the host Senators, tied, 3–3, in the 12th inning, Giant pitcher Jack Bentley was in a groove. But with one out in the inning, the Giants let the game get away. The Senators' Muddy Ruel, who had had only one hit in seven games, lifted a harmless foul behind the plate. Hank Gowdy, the Giant catcher, stepped into his discarded mask and fell to the ground. Ruel took advantage of his second chance by doubling to left field. Earl McNeely, the next hitter, bounced a ball to third; but it struck a pebble and ricocheted over Freddie Lindstrom's head for the game-winning and Series-winning hit.

Bentley should have been out of the inning in one-two-three style. Instead, he was the loser in the decisive game of the World Series.

*　*　*

Observe the way that Carlton Fisk of the White Sox handles foul pops. He holds on to the mask until the very last second; he then routinely flips it in a backward direction and easily makes the play.

"Don't s...w...i...n...g!"

The Element of Surprise

The Yankees are at bat with a runner on third base.

With a count of two balls and two strikes on the batter, the runner on third tries to steal home. The batter, totally surprised, takes the pitch which the umpire calls a ball. Meanwhile the runner is tagged out.

What's wrong with that play?

*   *   *

The runner never—repeat *never*—tries to steal home with two strikes on the batter. A hitter, when he has two strikes on him, has to protect the plate. So if the ball is close, he has to swing. If he does, the runner could be hit by either the ball or the bat. In either eventuality, the consequences could be disastrous.

* * *

The Yankees were guilty of that mistake a few years ago. Roy Smalley was the runner; Graig Nettles, the batter. Don Zimmer was the third-base coach. With a count of two balls and one strike, Nettles jumped out of the way of a pitch under his chin. Zimmer and Smalley assumed that the pitch was a ball, but the umpire called it a strike. On the next pitch, Zimmer thought that the count was three-one, instead of two-two, and he sent Smalley in.

Realizing the situation, Smalley, while running home, was pleading, "Graig, Graig, please don't swing."

Nettles didn't. But the strategy definitely took the possibility of a hit away from Nettles.

Switch-Hitting Strikeout

Rod Carew of the Angels is batting left-handed and runs a no-ball, two-strike count against a tough lefty, Ron Guidry of the Yankees. Then Carew pulls a surprise. He switches to batting right-handed.

Can he do this?

* * *

Yes. A batter can hit from both sides of the plate during the same at-bat.

* * *

Jimmy Piersall, playing for the White Sox in 1960, hit from both sides of the plate during the same at-bat. Batting righty, he took a strike. Then he switched to the left side and did the predictable thing—he struck out.

The Reckless Runner

With a runner on third base with no out in the fifth inning of a 3–3 game, the batter hits a two-hopper to first base. The runner breaks for home and becomes an easy out, first baseman to catcher.

Why is that bad baseball?

*   *   *

A runner at third with no out should never try to score on a ground ball unless he knows he can make it safely. With one out, the same principle applies. Runners on second and third follow the same rules. If there are runners on first and third, however, the advance runner should try to run home with no out, or one out, if the defense has a chance to turn a double play. In that case, one out is better than two.

*   *   *

In 1984 that play occurred in a Dodger-Cub game. Mariano Duncan, the rookie, was the Dodger runner at third. On a sharply hit ball to first base, Duncan broke for home, but was easily thrown out.

Why should Duncan not have gone home on the play? There was no out. The Dodgers' hottest hitters, Pedro Guerrero and Greg Brock, were coming up; and the first baseman was playing up on the grass.

It was simply a rookie mistake.

An Aggressive Mistake

The batter opens the seventh inning with a line-drive double down the left-field line.

Knowing that the opposing team is winning, 7–6, the batter realizes the importance of his run. As he approaches second, he sees the ball bouncing freely in the left-field corner; so he decides to gamble, hoping that if he reaches third safely, he will be in position to score on an outfield fly. He also knows that the left fielder has a bad arm. The risk, he thinks, is worth taking. But the left fielder makes a quick recovery and throws a perfect one-hop peg to the third baseman to beat the sliding runner.

Was the mistake in judgment the fault of the runner or of the third-base coach?

* * *

The blunder was the runner's. When he neared second, he sighted the left fielder and the ball. Judging that he could beat the throw to third, he sped up at that point. By the time he picked up the coach's signal, he had committed himself to advancing the extra base. There was no way that the coach could have stopped him. When the play is in front of the runner, the player, not the coach, makes the decision to run or to hold.

* * *

Steve Sax, who is older and more experienced than teammate Mariano Duncan, made such a base-running mistake in 1984. Sax led off an inning of a close game with a double to left, gambled on the extra base, and lost. He made an error in judgment. Let's call it an aggressive mistake. Some managers like to force the defense to make mistakes.

But a cardinal rule of baseball is, "Never make the first or the last out at third base."

Bigger Is Better

A young long-ball hitter is coming off a big season in which he has hit 40-plus home runs. Big and strong, he thinks that if he uses a longer and heavier bat, he will hit more home runs.

We know by now that pine tar cannot exceed 18 inches from the handle to the barrel. Is there a limit to the length of a bat?

* * *

Yes, a bat cannot exceed 42 inches in length. If it does, the batter who uses it is swinging an illegal bat. If he is detected, he is called out by the plate umpire.

* * *

Babe Ruth supposedly used a bat that weighed 48 ounces. The present average is about 34 ounces. There is usually just a one-number difference between the length and the weight of the bat. The Babe may have been using a 47-inch bat.

When the legendary Babe Herman first had a try-out with the Tigers, he carried along with him a pair of favorite bats that weighed approximately 45 ounces apiece. Ty Cobb, then the Tigers' manager, lifted one of the war clubs and said, "Why, even Babe Ruth's bats don't weigh this much."

Herman, who compared himself favorably with the other Babe, replied, "I know, but I figure if I use heavier bats than Ruth, I'll hit the ball further than him."

His theory was all wrong. Stan Musial swung a 31-ounce bat. He hit 475 major-league home runs. Distance, Musial said, is determined by speed of swing and speed of pitch. Of course, Musial knew that there were variables, such as wrists, weight, and balance.

Babe Ruth liked a heavy bat, Stan Musial a light one.

But obviously a hitter can swing a 31-ounce bat faster than he can swing a 45-ounce club.

Caught with the evidence.

Caught with the Evidence

A long-ball hitter for the White Sox listens to a fan who says he can improve the player's distance with a corked bat. The player feels that he has nothing to lose, so he goes along with the suggestion.

The fan saws two inches off the handle of the bat. He then stuffs cork down the middle of it. Then he glues the top back on. In closing, he says that the glue is unbelievably good: it will never come off.

In his first at-bat with his new piece of lumber, the player hits a long homer. In his second at-bat, he hits the ball one way for a base hit, but he sees the barrel of the bat go the other way.

What is the umpire's call?

* * *

The White Sox batter is called out for using an illegal bat.

*   *   *

Graig Nettles of the Yankees once lost a base hit exactly that way. Nettles, who felt like a fool, admitted his guilt. He said that a rule's a rule. You couldn't say, though, that he was a stickler for the rules.

Double Jeopardy

Let's change the last situation a little bit. Suppose that with one out, Nettles doesn't get a hit when his sawed-in-half bat flies apart. Instead, he lines the ball to Oriole shortstop Cal Ripken.

Yankee runner Lou Piniella is leading off second base at the time. Ripken, after he catches the ball, throws it to second baseman Rich Dauer, catching Piniella before he can get back. It's a double play. Or isn't it?

Is the inning really over?

*   *   *

Yes, the inning is really over. When Nettles hits with that illegal bat, any outs that occur as a result of the irregular at-bat count. It's not the same as batting out of order or interference.

So there was an inning-ending double play.

It Could Have Been

How important is it that a pitcher be able to cover first base well? It's ultra-important. It's so important that it might have cost the Yankees the 1985 pennant.

In this case, the Yankee pitcher breaks to his left on a ball hit to the first baseman. The throw is in time. But the pitcher, who had run directly across to the bag, overruns the bag in his haste to beat the runner. The ball then comes loose from his glove and rolls down the right-field line. Two Blue Jays score as the game turns around.

What mistake did the pitcher make?

* * *

The pitcher should have "bellied" into the catch. That is, he should have run to a spot on the foul line midway between home and first and cut to his left, running parallel to and inside the foul line. Then, he could have caught the ball while his right foot could be touching the second-base side of the base. In that way the pitcher avoids contact with the runner and makes the play the safe way.

* * *

Ron Guidry had outduelled Dave Stieb in the first game of the big September series with the pennant at stake, and it looked as though the Bronx Bombers were going to finally overtake the Blue Jays. But this basic play turned the game—and perhaps the season—around.

Don Mattingly, one of the best fielding first basemen in recent memory, made the play going to his right, turned and threw. Mattingly made a high throw, very uncommon for him. Phil Niekro, an accomplished fielder, in running straight towards the bag, got his hands up slowly. Normally he would have made that play. When the ball bounced off the pitcher's glove and trickled into the dugout, it allowed two runs to score.

Those runs decided the game, preventing Niekro from winning his 300th career victory and stopping the Yankees from creeping to one-half game from the American League lead.

The Yankees went on to lose eight consecutive games and were virtually eliminated from the race.

If he had made that play, he would have won his 300th game, and the Yankees *might* have won the pennant.

That's how important it is for a pitcher to be able to cover first base!

Everything to Gain

Suppose that Pete Rose, who is known for his hustle, is on first for the Reds with two out.

The batter hits a long fly ball to right field. Rose breaks with his teammate's contact. Just about everyone in the park thinks that the ball is foul. But a strong wind pulls the ball back into fair territory. The ball lands right inside the foul line as Rose, who never stopped running, scores from first on the play.

What's the moral?

* * *

Run hard on every play, especially if you've got nothing to lose. In this case, it turns out that Rose had everything to gain.

* * *

Actually, the Yankees' Steve Kemp was the real-life hero of this script. He scored on a wind-blown fly ball hit by Don Baylor.

Asked why he was running all-out on the play, he said, "There were two outs. I had nothing to lose."

My kind of ballplayer.

The Second Squeeze

The Yankees and the Oakland Athletics are tied in the bottom of the ninth. Dave Winfield is on third base with one out; Bobby Meacham is the batter.

Tommy John, the A's pitcher, suspects a squeeze bunt is planned and throws a pitchout to catcher Mike Heath. Winfield breaks with the pitch, but is frozen in his tracks when Meacham throws his bat at the wide pitch and misses.

Heath runs Winfield back to third, but throws the ball too soon, and too high, to Tony Phillips. Winfield anticipates the early throw and breaks past Heath for home. Phillips, who had caught the catcher's throw off-balance, rushes his throw to Tommy John, who is covering at home; but the throw is high and to the foul territory side of home plate. Winfield avoids John's tag and scores the winning run.

How do you score the winning run? Steal? Error?

*   *   *

There is no error charged on the play. Though it doesn't seem right, Winfield is credited with a steal of home. It wasn't his intent to steal home; but because he was in motion with the pitch, he is credited with the steal of home. Intent, as a matter of fact, has nothing to do with this play. Tommy John didn't intend to let Winfield score—and did everything within his power to prevent him from doing so—but due to two bad throws by fellow teammates, he was victimized by the loss and by the "theft" of home, which was charged to his record!

The Athletics conquered the suicide squeeze, but they got burned on the run-down play. The Yankees got burned on the squeeze attempt, but they beat the run-down play.

☺ 4 ☺

FAIR IS FAIR

The Fair Foul

Suppose the host Padres, in the bottom of the ninth inning, are tied with the Cubs.

The Padres' shortstop leads off the inning with a single to right. The Cubs look for the bunt, but the hitter slaps a single past the drawn-in infield. The next batter moves the runners up a base with a sacrifice bunt.

The Cubs elect to pitch to the Padres' power hitter. He slaps a soft fly ball down the left-field line. The Cub left-fielder thinks that he can catch the ball and hold the runner at third. But the ball bounces off the fingers of the left-fielder's glove, in fair territory, into foul territory for the game-winning hit.

The Cubs argue, however, that since the ball landed in foul territory, the umpire must call it foul. Is it?

* *. *

No, the Cubs are wrong. The determining factor is where the ball was touched. In this case, the ball was touched within the chalk lines, so it's a fair ball. Sometimes a fielder will be in fair territory, but touch and drop the ball while reaching across the chalk line into foul territory. In that instance, the ball is foul. At other times the fielder may be in foul territory, but touch and drop the ball while leaning over the foul line into fair territory. In that instance, the ball is fair.

*   *   *

In 1984 the Yankees encountered that problem in Milwaukee. In a tie game, in the bottom of the ninth, first baseman Mike Felder led off the inning with a single. The Yankee infield, expecting Paul Molitor to bunt, was surprised when the third baseman singled Felder to second. Randy Ready then sacrificed the runners to second and third, respectively.

The Yankees, with lefty Dave Righetti on the mound, elected to pitch to dangerous Cecil Cooper, a left-handed hitter. Cooper hit a Righetti fast ball down the left-field line. The left fielder attempted to make the play, but he deflected the ball, in fair territory, into foul ground, where it bounced. In the meantime, Felder scored the winning run.

Yankee manager Billy Martin argued wildly that the ball was touched in foul territory, so it should be a foul ball. But the umpire disagreed and stuck by his decision.

It's a good thing that he did. The video replay showed that the ball was touched in fair territory.

Fair ball. Fair call.

Foul's Fair

With a runner on first, a Blue Jay batter tops a hit at home plate. The ball bounces foul and spins out in front of the plate. The Tiger catcher pounces on the ball and fires it to the shortstop, who throws to first base for a double play.

The Blue Jays contend that the ball should be called foul, since it touched foul territory before it spun into the playing area. The Tigers insist that the play should stand as a double play.

Who is right?

*   *   *

The Tigers are right. As long as the ball has not passed first or third, it doesn't matter where the ball starts out; it matters where the ball is first touched.

If the batted ball *strikes* either the hitter, the catcher, the umpire, or any object in the batter's box, or foul territory, before rolling fair, it is a foul ball. If it doesn't hit a person or object in that area, and it spins fair, it is a fair ball. Conversely, if the ball lands fair and rolls foul before it is touched, and before it reaches first or third base, it is a foul ball.

A few years ago, that play occurred in a game at Baltimore.

*   *   *

Boston's Rick Burleson led the game off with a single to center against the Orioles' Mike Flanagan. The number-two batter topped the ball down in the batter's box. But it spun out in front of the plate. Catcher Rick Dempsey scooped the ball up and started the "double play."

In that instance, however, it wasn't ruled a double play. The umpire, who was screened off the play by Dempsey, saw the ball bounce once, when it landed foul. So he called the batted ball foul.

Even the umpires miss a call once in a while. But that missed call didn't make that home-plate umpire overly popular with Oriole manager Earl Weaver for the rest of that night.

✪ 5 ✪

THE UMPIRE RULES
SUPREME

The Four-Out Inning

Is it possible to make four legal outs in one inning?

Let's say the Angels have a man on third, another on second, and their star slugger is the batter with one out. The Twins' outfield is playing deep, so when the slugger loops a ball to shallow right field, the two runners take off. The Twins' right fielder gets a good jump on the ball, however, and he makes an outstanding catch. Without tagging up, the runner on third crosses the plate, and the outfielder's throw to the second baseman easily doubles up the runner from second for the third out.

Does the run count?

*   *   *

The run counts. It would not have counted if the Twins had been thinking, though. The rules say that a defensive team has the right to appeal a play at any time before either another play is started or all the infielders coming in have crossed the foul line. If the Twins had made an appeal in time on the runner at third, he would have become the *fourth* legal out. More importantly, an appeal would have nullified the Angel run. As it was, the plate umpire had to let the run stand, even though the third-base runner had not tagged up on the play.

* * *

An oversight of this kind could have cost the Houston Astros the 1980 pennant. In that year's playoffs, the Phillies had a runner on third, Mike Schmidt on first, and one out. The batter hit a looper to right field that looked as though it would fall safely. Both runners broke on the batter's contact with the ball. The right fielder made a fantastic running catch, however. Before he released the throw, to double-up Schmidt at first, the runner crossed the plate.

Houston, instead of requesting an appeal from the umpire at third, was happy to get out of the inning and thought the Phillies' run would not count. The Astros cleared the field. Then the plate umpire, who had made no prior signal, gave a sign to the official scorer that the run counted. Fortunately, the run had no bearing on the outcome of the game.

But, yes, it is possible to have four legal outs in one inning.

Pine-Tar Plays

Thurman Munson of the Yankees has just driven home a run in a 1975 game against the Twins.

But the Twins' manager appeals the play, claiming that Munson has too much pine tar on his bat. (The rules permit up to 18 inches of pine tar, from the handle to the barrel, to be applied to the bat.) Upon examination, the umpires find that the pine tar significantly exceeds the maximum limit.

What do the umpires rule?

* * *

Well, first they look at the rule book. When they find that this particular rule is not specifically covered by the text, they have to look up indirect references that help them form a conclusion. The references that they find are: 1) a batter will be out when he hits an illegally batted ball; 2) an illegally batted ball is one that is hit with a bat that does not conform to the rules; and 3) the bat handle may be covered with any foreign material, including pine tar, to improve the grip, as long as it does not exceed 18 inches from the knob to the barrel.

If, in the umpire's opinion, the foreign substance exceeds the 18-inch limit, the arbiter shall remove the bat from the game. Based upon that information, the umpires conclude that the bat was illegal and Munson is out. "A rule is a rule," they say, and the Yankees do not appeal.

* * *

Later, of course, there was the more famous "pine-tar incident" at Yankee Stadium in 1983.

The Royals were trailing the Yankees, 3–2, in the top of the ninth. With two out, and no one on base, U. L. Washington singled off reliever Goose Gossage, and George

Brett followed with an upper-deck homer that gave the Royals a 4–3 lead.

The Yankees filed an appeal, which the umpires upheld. Brett was called out for using an illegal bat. So New York left the field with an apparent 3–2 victory. But the Royals protested to the American League president.

Does the American League president uphold the protest?

The American League president, Lee McPhail, *does* uphold the protest. He says that while the umpires' decision was technically correct, it wasn't in keeping with the "spirit of the rules." The game has to be replayed with two out in the ninth inning.

The rules say that a batter shall be declared out if a tampered bat increases the distance of a batted ball. Pine tar, it is said, does not add distance to a batted ball.

Later in the season, the suspended game was completed. The Royals won, 4–3.

"Are you sure that's half a yard?"

The Fake-Out

Let's suppose that in the top of the 15th inning, in a game between Minnesota and Chicago, the Twins take a one-run lead.

But in the bottom half of the inning, Chicago's right fielder singles with one out. Then on a long fly ball, he tags up and runs to second. It is obvious to almost everyone in the ball park, including the runner, that he had left first too soon.

The Indian manager comes out to the mound to show the relief pitcher how to properly appeal the play. The pitcher takes his stretch, steps off the rubber, and, instead of throwing to first for the appeal, looks at second. When the runner sees the hurler look at second, he fakes a run to third. The pitcher reacts by faking the runner back to second.

What effect does the fake have on the appeal at first?

* * *

The Indian pitcher cannot now make an appeal at first. When he bluffs a throw to second, he forfeits his legal right to make an appeal play at first.

* * *

In a real 15-inning contest in the American League, the Brewers tried to come from behind against the Indians.

Charlie Moore, the runner, left too soon on a fly ball. After the ball was returned to the infield, Cleveland manager Jeff Torborg went out to the mound to show pitcher Victor Cruz how to conduct an appeal. When Cruz looked at second, however, he forgot everything he was told. He bluffed a throw to catch Moore at second and thereby lost the right to appeal at first.

No appeal play, no out.

The Run Stealer

Sometimes, though a runner misses a base, he can change a negative into a positive.

Let's say one man is at first base, with a runner in front of him at second, in a game at Detroit. There are two out. A Tiger batter lines a single to left center. One run scores and the hitter ends up on third. But he missed touching second. Both the Brewers and the Tigers know it.

The Brewers appeal the play. But, as the Brewers' pitcher steps off the rubber, the runner dashes for home. The pitcher throws to the catcher just in time to nip the speedy runner.

What mistake did the pitcher make?

* * *

The pitcher should have thrown the ball to second. If he had continued his appeal play, the runner would have been out at second, and no run would have scored. As it is, the runner is called out at the plate, the inning is over, but one run counts. Give the runner credit for a heads-up play. He is the reason why one run scores. If he had been safe at home, he would have scored another run.

* * *

In an actual game, Ron LeFlore of the Tigers got credit for that identical heads-up play against the Brewers. After he had missed second and was on third, the Brewers, appealing, put the ball in play. As their pitcher turned to throw to second, LeFlore broke for home. The startled pitcher broke his stride toward second, whirled, and fired to his catcher just in time to nip the runner.

LeFlore had nothing to lose. He was already out at second. If he had beaten the throw to home plate, he would have scored a second run for the Tigers.

The Infield (?) Fly

The Tigers, with men on second and first, have no out in the top of the eighth inning. The batter lofts a soft fly ball behind second base. The center fielder of the Brewers comes in; the second baseman goes out. Either one of them can catch the ball easily.

When the umpire sees the second baseman settle under the ball, he calls the batter automatically out on the infield fly rule. But the fielder drops the ball, and other players on the field lose their train of thought. The runner on second, believing the batter is safe on the error, runs to third, thinking that he is forced. The second baseman's throw beats him to the base, but the third baseman commits an error, too. He doesn't tag the runner. Instead, he steps on third for the "force."

Three questions: 1) Can an umpire call the infield fly rule when the defensive man is in the outfield? 2) Who gets charged with errors on the play? 3) Is the runner called back from third base?

Third, the runner on third base is not called back to second. In an infield fly play, the runner can advance at his own risk.

* * *

First, the umpire can call the infield fly rule on an outfield play. The rule permits the umpire to make the call any time the infielder can make the play with *ordinary* effort.

Second, there were two errors on the play: one of commission (the second baseman's) and one of omission (the third baseman's). However, since the second baseman's error confused the runner into running, he is charged with a miscue by the official scorer.

* * *

66

That play occurred in a 1956 game between the Braves and the Pirates. The Braves, with Frank Torre at bat, had Bobby Thomson on second and Bill Bruton on first. Pirate Dick Groat, an MVP winner four years later, dropped the ball and threw it to third baseman Gene Freese in time for the out. But Freese didn't tag Thomson; so the runner at third was safe, and Bruton moved up to second on the play.

There were three errors on the play: Groat's, Thomson's, and Freese's. But only Groat got officially charged with one.

The Pirates won the game, though, 3–1.

Not often is the league president in the stands when something peculiar happens.

It's Not Over Till It's Over

Is it possible to come to the plate three times in one at-bat and to get credited with just one official trip to the plate.

Hypothetically, the Cubs lead the Reds, 4–1, in the ninth inning. Cincinnati's star batter is at the plate with two out and no one on base. He hits a long fly ball that is fouled into the right-field stands. Before the next pitch, however, the ball falls onto the field. The shortstop calls time, but the Cub pitcher throws the ball to the batter. The batter flies out to center field and the game appears to be over. The third-base umpire says that the game is not over, though. He informs the Cub manager that his shortstop had called time.

The slugger bats again and singles, but the Cubs find out that they don't have a first baseman. The first sacker had gone directly to the dressing room when the batter had flown out the first time. The defensive team has to have nine men on the field, so the slugger has to bat a third time. This time he flies out to center, and the game is finally over.

If you were the manager of either team, would you have filed a protest somewhere during that bizarre at-bat?

*   *   *

Well, in real life, the manager of the team at bat protested before the hitter batted the third time when he should not have; and the skipper of the team on defense protested after the hitter's third at-bat.

You're probably wondering why the winning manager would protest after the batter hit into the game-ending out. Well, he had a reason. Read on.

Jeff Leonard was the actual Astro batter in the Mets' 4–1 win. In his first at-bat he flied out to Lee Mazzilli. The second time, he singled to left. Second baseman Doug Flynn took the relay throw and whirled to fire to first. To his surprise, he didn't see a first baseman.

That's because there wasn't one. Ed Kranepool had gone to the clubhouse after Leonard's fly to Mazzilli. The umpires called Leonard back to the plate a third time. But Houston manager Bill Virdon protested, saying that the Astros shouldn't be penalized for the Mets' mistake. Leonard flied out again, ending the game. Or so most people thought.

But after the game National League president Chub Feeney, who had been at the ball park that day, upheld the Astro protest. The next day, Joe Torre of the Mets protested

Feeney's decision. But Met pitcher Kevin Kobel retired Jose Cruz to end the game—and the controversy.

Leonard came out ahead, though. He got credited with a base hit, instead of a fly out.

And, yes, it is possible to come to the plate three times in one at-bat and to get credited with just one official at-bat.

The Umpire Always Wins

The batter takes a pitch that is called a strike. The hitter disagrees with the call. The hurler pitches again and the batter takes again. The umpire calls another strike. By this time, the batter who is furious with the umpire's calls against him, steps out of the batter's box and argues vigorously. The umpire orders him to resume his hitter's position. He refuses.

What does the umpire do?

*   *   *

The umpire orders the pitcher to throw the ball. The arbiter calls an automatic strike for every pitch that is made while the hitter is out of the batter's box. At any time, the hitter can step into the box and resume the count from that point.

*   *   *

Frank Robinson, when with the Reds, got called out on such a play in 1956, his rookie year. He argued about a called second strike in a game against the Giants. Umpire Larry Goetz told him to get back in the box. Robinson refused.

Goetz ordered the Giants' Steve Ridzik to pitch, and called "Strike three" while Robinson was still disputing the previous call!

What's the Pitch?

In a hypothetical case, the star hitter of the Red Sox is on third base, with the next batter at the plate.

When the Texas pitcher goes into his windup, the third-base umpire calls, "Balk!" But the hurler pitches the ball anyway and the batter bloops a double to left. The runner on third, who had heard the umpire call a balk, remains on third. The batter who hit the double clutches second. In fact, he refuses to leave the base.

How does the umpire resolve this predicament?

*   *   *

Once again, the balk takes precedence; so the umpire lets the runner from third score and returns the batter to the plate. When the batter refuses to leave second base, the umpire ejects him from the game, and places his substitute at the plate.

*   *   *

In a real-game situation, Lou Piniella of the Yankees, who relished every hit he ever got, refused to leave second under similar circumstances. He had to be kicked out of the game before he would give up his double.

"Get up off second base . . . you don't own it."

The Cunning Catcher

The Mets' catcher is noted for thinking all the time. The following hypothetical example points it out:

The Braves' clean-up hitter is at bat with a man on first, one out, and a three-two count on him. As the Mets' hurler pitches, the runner breaks for second. The batter checks his swing and the plate umpire calls, "Ball four!" The Braves' first-base coach yells to the runner to stand up. But the catcher throws to second anyway; and the Mets' second baseman makes an easy tag on the runner, who has slowed down.

Then the Mets appeal the swing. The first-base umpire says the batter broke his wrists, which constitutes a swing. Strike three.

Is it a double play?

* * *

No, it is not a double play. The runner cannot be penalized for the umpire's mistake. The runner, misled by the false signal, slows down. But there is no guarantee that the runner would have stolen the base had he run hard all the way. The umpire calls the batter out, but puts the runner back on first.

Thurman Munson of the Yankees was such a catcher. In the mid-1970's, he pulled off the identical play. He thought he should have had a double play.

On defense, as an offense, Munson was always thinking one out ahead of the game.

Not on My Time

An artful base runner finds himself caught in a run-down in a game. Knowing that there is no chance to escape, he turns to the umpire and requests, "Time."

Does the umpire grant it?

*   *   *

No, the umpire does not grant it. A request for time out must either precede or succeed a play. When the runner, in this case, is tagged, he is called out.

A player who made this actual request in a game was Ellis Valentine of the Mets. It drew snickers from the opposition and a belly laugh from the umpire.

But the end result, Met or no-Met, was, "You're out!"

Don't bite when the pitch is a floater.

Home Run Chase

A well-known slugger is batting against a pitcher who hasn't been having too much success recently against him.

The hurler decides to throw a floater. The pitch is too tempting for the batter to let go, so he runs up on the ball and, with his front foot out of the batter's box, hits the pitch for a home run.

Is it a legal one?

*   *   *

No, the home run is not legal. The batter must have both feet within the box when he makes contact with the ball. If he hits a ball with one, or both, of his feet outside of the box, he is considered to have hit a ball illegally, and he is called out. It is important to note, however, that if the batter misses the pitch, it is simply a strike and he continues to hit.

*   *   *

Hank Aaron lost a home run in this fashion. He "chased" a pitch by Cardinal left-hander Curt Simmons and homered into an out.

Aaron has an all-time high 755 career home runs. One more wouldn't have made too much difference.

Teamwork

The Red Sox have a runner at third base, and one out.

The batter hits a long fly ball to right center against the Yankee pitcher. The ball deflects off the right-fielder's glove and floats into the center fielder's mitt.

Two questions: 1) Is the batter out? and 2) can the runner tag up after the ball touches the right-fielder's glove?

*   *   *

A fly ball that is deflected off one outfielder's glove into another one's is a legal out. The batter is out.

A runner can legally tag up and advance as soon as a fielder touches the ball. He does not have to wait until a fielder "possesses" the ball.

*   *   *

On a play just like this, at Yankee Stadium in the late 1950's, Hank Bauer got the assist and Mickey Mantle, the putout. There was no runner on third.

The batter got "put out."

Passed Ball, Passed Chance

A runner is on third base with the bases loaded and two out. The batter strikes out for what seems to be the third out, but the pitch gets away from the catcher.

The runner on third, who doesn't seem to understand the situation, stays at third while the batter takes off for first. The catcher retrieves the ball and throws late to first. In the meantime, prodded by his third-base coach, the runner sets off for home. But the first baseman's return throw to the catcher gets there in time, and the catcher tags the runner for the third out.

Was the batter out when he missed the third strike? Did the catcher have to throw the ball to first? Did the catcher have to tag the oncoming runner?

*   *   *

The batter is not out when he misses the third strike. The batter automatically becomes a runner when the third strike called by the umpire is not caught, provided 1) first base is unoccupied, or 2) first base is occupied with two out.

The catcher did not have to throw the ball to first. He could just have stepped on home with the ball in hand for the force play, if he could have beaten the runner to the plate, or he could have thrown to the pitcher, who should have been covering the plate.

And he did not have to tag the runner.

*   *   *

Several years ago, Bill Russell, a veteran of many years with the Dodgers, pulled that base-running blunder. In a similar situation, at Veterans Stadium in Philadelphia, he did not know that a batter can become a runner if the third strike is not caught with two out.

The catcher threw late to first baseman Pete Rose, who knew exactly what to do. Rose threw to the catcher, who tagged Russell out at the plate.

Once again, the tag was not necessary.

Lift cap, scratch head, spit on hands, lift bat, knock dirt out of cleats, rub hands . . . then step in batter's box.
"Have I covered everything?"

The Costly Call

Carlton Fisk of the White Sox ordinarily takes a long time to get into the batter's box. One night, as he goes through his pre-batter's-box routine, the plate umpire spots Yankee pitcher Dave Righetti committing a balk, and calls it.

Is the call a correct one?

*   *   *

No, the umpire makes a bad call here. Righetti, even though he made an illegal move, cannot be called for a balk if the hitter isn't in the batter's box. The umpire should have been watching Fisk, first, and Righetti, second.

When Righetti was called for a balk before Fisk stepped into the batter's box, it was not only a wrong call, but a costly one, causing the Yankees a loss, as it happened.

Inside the Lines

Suppose the Red Sox are at bat with runners on second and first with no out in a game against the White Sox.

The batter drops a bunt down the first-base line. The White Sox catcher picks the ball up and throws it to the first baseman. But the batter, who is running inside the first-base line, is hit by the throw. The ball bounds down the right-field line, allowing the runner on second to score. That run turns out to be the deciding one.

Does it count?

*   *   *

The run shouldn't count, if the umpire sees the play the same way we do. In running the last 45 feet to first base,

"That's *my* elbow."

the batter-runner has to run within the three-foot line that parallels the base line for that distance. If he is hit by the throw when *inside* or *outside* that area, he should be called out and the ball declared dead.

*   *   *

This controversial play occurred in the 1969 World Series between the Mets and the Orioles. With runners on first and second, no out, and a tied game in the bottom of the tenth inning, J. C. Martin, the Mets' batter, dropped a bunt down the first-base line.

Pete Richert, the pitcher for the Orioles, fielded the ball and threw it to first. Martin was running inside the first-base line. The throw hit Martin on the arm and bounced into foul territory while Jerry Grote of the Mets sprinted home with the winning run.

Most observers thought that Martin was clearly out of the base lines and should have been declared out. The umpire saw the play differently, however. His was the vote that counted.

The Mets' run counted, too.

A Catchy Situation

The Reds and Red Sox are tied 1–1 in the bottom half of the ninth inning. In Game 3 of the 1975 World Series, they are also tied at one game apiece.

Cesar Geronimo leads off the Reds' inning with a bloop single. Then the next batter drops down a bunt right in front of the plate. But he is slow to move out of the batter's box. Red Sox catcher Carlton Fisk has to shove the batter out of the way with his glove hand and pick the ball up with his bare hand. Fisk's throw beats Geronimo by plenty of time at second; but because of the bodily contact at the plate, his off-balance throw goes into center field. Geronimo continues to third. The Red Sox want the batter to be called out for interference. In fact, they want two outs, for that's what they would have gotten, if Fisk's throw were on the mark.

What did they get?

* * *

They got nowhere. The plate umpire disallowed the appeal, claiming that the contact was accidental, not purposeful. Joe Morgan, the next batter, singled, Geronimo scored, and the game was over.

* * *

That play might have cost the Red Sox the 1975 World Series. The Reds went on to win the World Series in seven games. Had the call gone the other way, the Red Sox might have won Game 3. If they had, they would have won the World Series in six games.

The Five-Minute Forfeit

The manager of the Dodgers, for example, takes exception to the presence of a tarpaulin in the Chicago bullpen. He claims that the tarpaulin poses a threat to his players, so he requests that the umpires have it removed. When the umpires refuse the request, the visiting manager removes his players from the field.

What do the umpires do?

* * *

Well, if the umpire is Marty Springstead, he gives the skipper five minutes to put his players back on the field. If he doesn't beat the deadline, the umpire forfeits the game to the Cubs.

* * *

Earl Weaver of the Orioles registered the same complaint in a 1977 game with the Blue Jays, who were winning 4–0 in the fifth inning. Springstead, after Weaver failed to make the five-minute deadline, forfeited the game to the Blue Jays.

That game was played on September 15. At that time, the Yankees were safely entrenched in first place. If Weaver's players had had a chance to win the pennant, you can be certain that he would have had his players positioned on the field before Springstead's deadline.

"Five minutes or forfeit!"

Stretching the Rules

Some pitchers like to work from the stretch in one continuous motion. The umpires "look the other way" as long as no one complains. But one day a batter got upset with the motion, so the umpires enforced the balk rule.

What exactly is the rule?

*   *   *

The umpires don't always agree on a balk. The pitcher, working from the stretch, must come to a set position before he releases the ball. That's what the rule book says.

*   *   *

In the early 1950's, a plate umpire called a record four balks on Yankee pitcher Vic Raschi in one game. Raschi didn't like to come to a stop position. After the umpire had called the first balk, Raschi became stubborn. The pitcher wanted to see how far the umpire would go. Raschi stopped committing balks only when manager Casey Stengel warned him that one more infraction would cost him money.

Allie Reynolds, who didn't like to come to a stop position, either, pitched the next day. When the first runner against him reached base, Reynolds paid undue attention to him. The pitcher kept on throwing to first base. Minutes went by. But he refused to deliver the ball to the plate. Finally the fans got restless. They began to boo.

The plate umpire got restless, too. He visited the mound and asked Reynolds why he wasn't pitching to the batter. Reynolds said that he was afraid that if he pitched the ball, the umpire would call a balk.

That ended the balk calls. Raschi and Reynolds continued to pitch to the plate in one fluid motion.

A Hit's a Hit

Suppose that Willie McGee, the National League batting title winner in 1985, gets five hits in a mid-season game at Chicago; but the game is called, with the score tied, because Wrigley Field does not have lights. The game, the league president says, is to be concluded at the end of the season.

Does McGee get credit for the hits at the time he gets them, or does he have to wait for the credit?

*   *   *

McGee will have to wait until the game is finalized before he *finally* gets credit for his hitting spree. Of course, if his name were Pete Rose, the situation might be different.

When Rose was in a countdown situation to Ty Cobb's once record 4,191 career hits, the Cincinnati player-manager participated in such a game at Wrigley Field. He got two, not five, hits, though. The baseball public didn't want Rose's hits put off to the end of the year, though. So Chub Feeney, the National League president, made an exception: he let that game's records, up to that point, count.

Normally, though, the game records would not count until there was a final *count* in the contest.

Caught in the Act

A veteran pitcher who has been known to "doctor" the baseball is pitching for Oakland. In the fifth inning the umpire suspects that a foreign substance was used on the previous pitch.

What should the umpire do?

* * *

The umpire should call the pitch a ball and warn the moundsman that if he throws another similar-type pitch, he will be ejected from the game.

Later in the game, the umpire sees the pitcher repeatedly touching the bottom part of the peak of his cap. The umpire calls, "Time," walks out to the mound, and, upon inspection, he finds the peak covered with grease.

What should the umpire do in this situation?

* * *

Any time that the umpire catches the pitcher with the goods—in this case, the "goo"—the hurler should be ejected from the game.

Surprisingly, there have been very few ejections for doctoring a baseball. Rick Honeycutt, then with the Mariners, got suspended for 15 days when an umpire found him with a thumbtack taped to his finger. Honeycutt used the thumbtack to scratch the cover of the ball.

Gaylord Perry of the Mariners was once ejected from a game, too. Early in the game, a Red Sox batter stepped out of the box and asked the plate umpire to look at the ball. The umpire found grease on the ball. But he couldn't eject Perry, because the hurler hadn't actually pitched the ball.

Later in the game, however, Perry found himself in a tough situation, pitching to Rick Miller. One of Perry's pitches came perfectly straight for 59 feet, then dropped two feet in the last foot.

"I wonder how it got that way."

Perry was ejected for "suspicion" of throwing a spitter. He was the first pitcher in almost *forty* years to be ejected for throwing that pitch.

The Trap-Ball Trap

Let's suppose there is a runner at first base with one out; the batter is hitting against the opponents' star pitcher.

The hitter loops a ball to right field, and the outfielder either catches it or traps it. One umpire calls the play a catch; another, a trap. The runner at first, who is confused, finally decides to run to second. One umpire calls him safe; the other umpire, out.

How do the umpires resolve this contradictory situation?

* * *

The umpires are in a tight spot on this one. The only way out is compromise. They allow the runner to stay at second, but call the batter out.

* * *

The Mets and the Reds had a similar situation. The Cincinnati outfielder made such a good try that he confused the umpires. He also confused the Met base runner.

The only way out, the umpires concluded, was to give a little and to take a little. Neither the Mets nor the Reds argued too long, since each got something: the Mets, a base; the Reds, an out.

Trapped Ball Call

In a key playoff game, the center fielder appears to make a shoestring catch off a line drive. But the nearby umpire rules a trap on the play as the lead run scores. But, two of the four umpires thought that the ball was caught.

Which umpire's call is the prevailing one?

*　　*　　*

The umpire who is working second base is the arbiter whose ruling carries clout on this particular play. He is the nearest umpire to the play.

*　　*　　*

This play created a great deal of controversy in the American League's playoffs in 1985. Lloyd Moseby, center fielder for Toronto, made such a play. Willie Wilson of the Royals, who was running from second with two outs, scored easily when the play was ruled a trap.

The second-base umpire had not seen the play clearly and indecisively called it a trapped catch. He instantly looked to the right-field umpire for help. The right-field umpire supported the second-base arbiter's call. Instant replay shots, on television, though not clear either, supported Moseby's claim that he had caught the ball cleanly.

The Blue Jays ended the controversy when they scored two runs in the bottom half of the inning to win the game.

End of Argument

As the runner comes sliding into second, the second baseman tags the runner with his gloved left hand, while he holds the ball in his right hand.

Is the runner out or safe?

*   *   *

He is safe. The fielder must tag the runner with the ball. He could tag him 1) with the ball in his glove, 2) with two hands, and 3) with the ball in his bare hand. But he cannot make a legal tag 1) with his glove, when the ball is not in it, or 2) with his bare hand, when the ball is not in it.

If there is a force situation, it doesn't matter which hand the ball is in, as long as the fielder touches second with his foot or any part of his body before the runner.

*   *   *

Gene Mauch, when he was the manager of the Expos, argued such a play at second base one day. He claimed that infielder Tim Foli had made a tag on the sliding runner in plenty of time. The umpire agreed, but pointed out that Foli had the ball in his other hand when he made the tag.

End of argument.

*   *   *

In the 1970 World Series there was a bizarre play at home plate. Bernie Carbo of the Reds slid home, but never reached the plate. Catcher Elrod Hendricks of the Orioles tagged Carbo with his glove, but the ball was in his bare hand. The umpire, who was out of position, didn't see either Carbo miss the plate or Hendricks miss the tag.

What call did he make? He called the runner out.

What call should he have made? He shouldn't have made any call. Carbo didn't reach the plate. The umpire couldn't call Carbo safe. Hendricks didn't tag Carbo. So the umpire couldn't call Carbo out.

Should he have asked another umpire. Yes, undoubtedly. But, on a judgment call, the umpire involved in the play may *request* another opinion. In this case, he didn't. He can't be overruled, unless he makes the request.

Bad Timing

The Mets' first batter of the inning flies out. The player who is supposed to follow him in the lineup holds back and another player steps up to the plate instead.

The manager of the Padres knows that this is not the proper batter; so he appeals while the wrong player is still batting.

Is this a proper appeal?

*   *   *

No, this appeal is not proper. The manager making an appeal must wait until the hitter completes his time at bat. Then, before a pitch is thrown to the next batter, the skipper must make his appeal.

*   *   *

Manager John McNamara of the Padres made this mistake. Bud Harrelson of the Mets was batting out of turn. When McNamara appealed on the spot, the appeal was denied and the Mets were allowed to substitute the "proper" hitter. But once again they sent up a hitter who was batting out of turn.

This time McNamara had the right appeal procedure committed to memory. The batter who was supposed to be hitting and was bypassed was called out.

Batting Out of Turn

The Dodgers flipped their batting order a few years ago. Usually Ron Cey followed Dusty Baker, but manager Tommy Lasorda switched them one night. With runners on first and third, Baker came up in Cey's turn, however, and hit into a force play.

Manager Dallas Green of the Phillies made the proper appeal. But he wanted two out, instead of one: one for the hitter batting out of turn and one for the force play. Did he get two outs?

*   *   *

No, he got only one out. Cey, who was supposed to be batting, was called out. Baker, who had hit into the force, was still the batter, since he followed Cey in the order. The runners were put back on first and third, since runners cannot be put out or score while an illegal batter is hitting.

The umpires at the time checked the rule book and found that there was nothing there to cover an out made during an illegal at-bat. (There is now.) But they reasoned that the base runners couldn't be put out by the actions of a player who wasn't supposed to be up.

94

⊗ 6 ⊗

WATCH YOUR STEP
AS YOU LEAVE

Merkle's Boner

Suppose we have this situation: Braves' runners are on first and second, and the score, Houston 5, Atlanta 5, in the bottom of the ninth inning. The Braves' star batter lines a two-out base hit that scores the runner on second with the apparent winning run.

The runner at first, seeing the lead run score without a throw, doesn't bother to touch second base. Instead, he heads straight for the clubhouse. The Astro second baseman, in the meantime, retrieves the ball and steps on second base for the force.

Is the game over? With what kind of hit is the batter credited?

*   *   *

The game continues with the score still tied. When a runner is in a force-play situation, he must touch the advance base before a run can score on a hit with two out. The runner who does not touch second is called out on the force. The batter does not get credit for either an RBI or a hit.

*   *   *

The Giants lost a pennant because of a player's failure to touch the advance base in that exact situation. Late in the 1908 season, first baseman Fred Merkle pulled a blooper when he failed to touch second base after Al Bridwell's apparent single had downed the Cubs and "clinched" the pennant for the Giants. But, in the midst of the pennant-winning celebration by the Giants, Johnny Evers, the Cubs' second baseman, retrieved the ball, touched second, and got the umpire to call Merkle out.

The game, which thereby ended in a tie, because the players had left the field and the fans had taken over, eventually had to be replayed because the Giants lost their last five games and ended the season in a tie with the Cubs. Chicago won the sudden-death matchup and earned the right to represent the National League in the World Series against the Tigers.

Since that time, the play has gone down in the history books as "Merkle's Boner." But obviously no one would remember the blooper today if the Giants had won just one of their last six games.

Heads-Down Plays

Harvey Haddix of the Pirates has pitched 12 consecutive perfect innings against the Braves. But the Bucs couldn't score against the Braves' Lew Burdette, either, so the score was 0–0 going to the 13th inning.

Inning number 13 proved unlucky for Haddix. An infield error, a sacrifice, and an intentional pass to Henry Aaron brought Joe Adcock up to the plate with two on and one out. Adcock "homered" over the right-center-field fence. But the "homer" turned out to be a double when Aaron, thinking that the ball was caught, headed for the dugout just before he reached third. Adcock, running with his head down, didn't see Aaron leave the base path and passed him. But before that, the runner from second crossed the plate. Does the run count?

* * *

Yes, the run counts. Adcock's out was only the second one of the inning. If it were the third, the run would still count, since the out was made after the runner from second had crossed the plate.

* * *

In 1931 Lou Gehrig tied Babe Ruth for the home run lead with 46 circuit clouts. He should have won the title with 47 round-trippers, though. Lyn Lary, a base runner when Gehrig hit a fence-clearing blow that summer, thought that the ball had been caught, too, and, between third and home, ran for the dugout. Gehrig, with his head down, too, passed Lary and could only be credited with a triple.

* * *

The 1985 final statistics show that Bobby Meacham of the Yankees failed to hit a home run until the last month of the season. But early in the season, he had hit a fence-clearing blow. He was so excited, though, that he passed a hesitant Willie Randolph between first and second.

Meacham was credited with a *single*.

Intent Breeds Discontent

Let's suppose the Red Sox have runners on third, second and first. There are two out and the batter has a three-two count on him.

The Blue Jays' star pitcher throws, the batter takes. The umpire signals strike three, but yells, "Ball four."

The runner on third, thinking that the inning is over, trots to the dugout as the Blue Jay catcher rolls the ball back to the mound. Suddenly there's a foot race. The runner from second races toward the plate; and the catcher, who realizes that the inning is still going on, retrieves the ball and lunges at the sliding runner, who evades the tag. The Red Sox runner, entering the dugout, notices the action on the field, exits from the dugout, and bolts for home. The catcher tags him out to end the inning.

The opposing managers demand an explanation; how does the plate umpire justify the confusion which his double call has caused?

* * *

Actually he should call the lead runner out for leaving the base path or the next runner out for passing on the base path. But in either case, he would be penalizing the Red Sox for his mistake. So he probably calls upon the "Compromise Rule," which gives something to each team. He allows one run to score but calls the lead runner out. Thus, the Red Sox get a run, and the Blue Jays get out of the inning.

* * *

That's exactly what happened when this zany sequence of events occurred in a game between the Dodgers and the Pirates.

Lee Lacy was on third; Jimmy Wynn, second; and another Dodger, first. Jerry Reuss was the Pirate pitcher; Manny Sanguillen, the catcher; and Joe Ferguson, the Dodger batter.

The umpire, in this case, called "Strike three," but he didn't mean it. He meant "Ball four." When Sanguillen heard "Strike three," he really thought the inning was over. He wasn't trying to take advantage of the umpire's mistake. That's why Sanguillen rolled the ball back to the mound. But then the arbiter directed Ferguson to go to first base, and the game to continue. In the outcome, a run did score.

That's when the fun started.

Manager Walter Alston of the Dodgers didn't fully understand what had happened, but he knew that he had gotten a "bum" deal. The walk, the proper call, would have given him a run and a live inning. But the umpire called upon the "Compromise Rule" to avoid a full-scale war.

A Rookie Mistake

A rookie for the Dodgers is at first base. The batter is the Dodgers' star outfielder. The hitter swings at a curve ball and loses his bat as he misses the pitch. The bat rolls down the first-base line in foul territory. The rookie, trying to be helpful, leaves his base to retrieve the bat and throws it to his veteran teammate, who is at the plate. The pitcher, who has taken the return throw from his catcher, fires the ball to his first baseman, who tags the rookie returning to the base.

Is the rookie out?

*   *   *

Yes, he is out. When the ball is live, the runner leaves his base at his own risk. The rookie was trying to be nice and helpful. But this is an example of Leo Durocher's saying: "Nice guys finish last."

*   *   *

Pee Wee Reese, of all people, made that mistake in his rookie year for the Dodgers. Dixie Walker, the veteran, lost his bat. Reese, trying to do the right thing, did the wrong thing: he retrieved the bat and got tagged out.

That was one of the few mistakes that Reese, a long-time Dodger captain, ever made on the ball field.

"Your bat, sir."

"I never wanted the outfield."

What's the Score?

A fast-racing outfielder appears to catch a looper hit into center field by the home-team's slugger, but the umpire rules that the speedster trapped the ball after it touched the grass.

The home-town fans, who are furious with the call, hurl objects, such as fruit and bottles, onto the field. Some of the missiles hit two of the umpires. When appeals to the fans, by way of the public address system, fail to quiet the angry spectators, it is evident that something drastic has to be done.

What drastic action do the umpires take?

*   *   *

The umpires, when they cannot quiet the rioting fans, who are dangerous to participants and spectators alike, must rule a forfeit. In this case, to the visiting team. The final score of a forfeit is 9–0. The award-winning team receives one run for every inning of a regulation game.

*   *   *

The Giants of 1949 picked up this type of forfeit when the fans at Connie Mack Stadium in Philadelphia could not be calmed down after an umpire ruled that Phillie center fielder Richie Ashburn had trapped a ball.

Ashburn was one of the greatest defensive center fielders of all time. The Phillie fans, we can suppose, thought that Ashburn could catch any ball which came near him.

Reverse Strategy

Take the case where the Cubs have a runner on second and another on first in the sixth inning, when the batter pops up to the Cardinals second baseman.

Since there is one out, the batter is automatically retired, because the infield fly rule is in effect. The second baseman drops the ball, however. So the runners are free to advance at their own risk. The Cub on second breaks for third, but is beaten by the throw to the third baseman, who steps on the base.

Are the Cardinals out of the inning?

*   *   *

The inning is still going, with Cub runners on first and third. Because the batter was automatically out on the infield fly, there is no force in effect. The third baseman has to tag the runner. He doesn't, so there are still two out.

*   *   *

In real life Ron Santo of the Cubs was the runner on second. Julian Javier of the Cardinals was the one who dropped the ball and threw it to Ken Boyer, who stepped on third base. Santo thought that he was out, however, and headed toward the dugout. Pitcher Ray Sadecki yelled to Boyer to tag Santo, which the Redbird third-sacker did when the Bruin tried to return to the bag.

Then the Cardinals were out of the inning.

7

LET THEM LAUGH

Who has the ball?

The Wayward Ball

A famous player drags a bunt down the first-base line. The pitcher fields the ball and lunges to tag him. But the pitcher loses control of the ball, and it rolls inside the shirt of the runner.

Now, seeing he is in control of the ball, the runner circles the bases while the infielders, in a state of confusion, don't know whether they should chase him or tackle him.

Does the run count?

* * *

No, the run doesn't count. When the ball becomes the possession of the runner, he is limited to the base to which he is advancing. So, he has to return to first base.

* * *

In 1933, Rabbit Maranville, reaching the end of a distinguished Hall-of-Fame career, laid down such a bunt and circled the bases while Dodger pitcher Van Lingle Mungo chased him indecisively from first to home.

The play caused some indecision on the umpires' part, too, and sent them scurrying to the rule book for a definition of the play.

One base.

"I never meant any harm."

Winfield Gets the *Bird*

A Yankee outfielder, playing against the host Blue Jays, is warming up between innings. Suddenly a sea gull lands on the grass, just a short distance away.

Not knowing the bird is wounded, he impulsively throws at it, believing that he does not have a chance of hitting it. But the bird, which doesn't move, is killed by the thrown ball.

What is the outfielder's punishment, if any?

* * *

Canadians have a fond feeling toward sea gulls. So, first, the legal authorities arrest the outfielder. Then the player posts a five-hundred-dollar bond and faces a cruelty-to-animal charge.

* * *

Dave Winfield, believe it or not, is the one who faced that charge in Toronto. He suffered a lot of bad publicity before he finally got absolved of the charge.

Since that time, he has limited his putouts to runners, not grounded flyers.

Too Tempting to Take

Suppose the Indians have a runner on second base with a good contact hitter at the plate? The batter smashes a single to center field; but on the one-hop throw to the plate from Seattle's outfielder, the on-deck hitter steps in front of the Mariner catcher and hits the throw deep to the outfield.

How would the home-plate umpire call this play, which was not specifically covered in the official baseball rules at the time?

*   *   *

The umpire would call the on-deck batter out for interference. That would be the second out of the inning. Also, he would not allow the runner from second to score. Instead, he would return the runner to third base, which he had safely made; and he would hold the batter-runner at first base.

*   *   *

You probably think that this unusual play could never happen in a real game. But it actually did.

The Indians once had an outfielder-first baseman by the name of Jay Kirke, who was a pretty good fast-ball hitter. But he couldn't touch a curve ball. Consequently, he saw nothing but breaking pitches.

After the game, he told reporters he couldn't help himself. He hadn't seen a fast ball in over a month. He just couldn't resist the temptation to swing.

"Who Said That?"

There is a three-two count on the batter with a runner on first. As the pitch comes in, the umpire at home plate hesitates a moment before calling "Strike three." The runner from first has started running with the pitch and coasts into second. Meanwhile the umpire there thinking the call was ball four, yells "Ball four." But when the catcher throws to second and the shortstop tags the runner out, the second-base umpire can only agree he's out. The plate umpire had called "Strike three" but so late that confusion ensued.

How does the second-base umpire explain that one to the runner?

* * *

The second-base umpire is Ron Luciano, who doesn't explain it to the runner directly.

Chet Lemon of the White Sox was the player who was victimized by that late call. He took the embarrassment in stride. He left the field without a complaint. When he ran out to his position, after his team had been put out, however, he asked Luciano who it was who yelled "Ball four."

Luciano, dodging the bullet, said "Campaneris," the A's shortstop.

The *Hip* Play

In the bottom of the sixth inning, the host Twins, who are trailing the Royals, 2–1, have runners on second and first with one out.

The Twins' batter hits a low liner to the left of the shortstop. The Royal shortstop drops the ball; then he picks it up, steps on second for the force play, and throws to the first baseman to try to complete the double play. But the throw hits the man running toward second (who has already been forced at second) on the hip and is deflected down the right-field line. The Twins' runner from second scores the tying run.

What's the call?

*   *   *

Well, there are many things to consider here. Did the shortstop deliberately drop the ball? Was the runner from first to second illegally in the base path? Did he deliberately obstruct the path of the ball?

If the umpire rules that the shortstop deliberately dropped the ball, the arbiter calls the batter out and the ball dead. He leaves the runners where they were before the play.

He rules that the runner is not guilty of being in the base path illegally.

If the umpire rules that the runner deliberately obstructed the throw, the batter-runner is called out, thus completing the inning-ending double play.

*   *   *

That identical play turned the 1978 World Series around. The Yankees' Thurman Munson was on second, Reggie Jackson was on first, and Lou Piniella was the batter. Dodger shortstop Bill Russell dropped Piniella's liner, forced Jackson at second, and fired to Steve Garvey at first.

The ball struck Jackson on the hip and rolled down the right-field line, allowing Munson to score and Piniella to take second.

The umpires ruled that 1) Russell did not deliberately drop the ball, 2) Jackson had a right to the base path, and 3) Jackson did not deliberately obstruct the throw to first base.

The Yankees, who at that time were down two-games-to-one in the Fall Classic, went on to win the game and the World Series.

But no one knows how the World Series might have turned out if the Dodgers had turned that double play.

Adding Insult to Injury

The Yankees' Don Baylor, who recently broke Minnie Minoso's American League record of being hit by pitched balls, is the batter; the Blue Jays' Doyle Alexander is the pitcher in a late season 1985 game.

With a count of two balls and one strike on the hitter, Alexander throws a slow curve on the inside part of the plate. Baylor, instead of jumping out of the way of the ball, twists his body to his right side, and moves his left shoulder into the flight of the ball, which hits him.

Does the umpire give Baylor first base?

* * *

If the umpire believes that Baylor made no effort to avoid the pitch, and/or he moved his body into the path of the ball, the answer is "no." Charge a strike to Baylor and make the count two-and-two. In this instance, the umpire awarded Baylor first base.

* * *

In 1968, when the Dodgers' Don Drysdale was going for the consecutive scoreless innings record, he got into trouble in the ninth inning, en route to his fifth straight shutout.

Dick Dietz of the Giants came to the plate with the bases loaded and no out. On a two-one count, Dietz turned his body into a slow breaking pitch. The umpire disallowed the free base, and charged a strike to Dietz's count.

Drysdale then retired Dietz and the following two Giant batters to keep his streak intact. He went on to set the record by posting 58 and two-thirds consecutive scoreless innings.

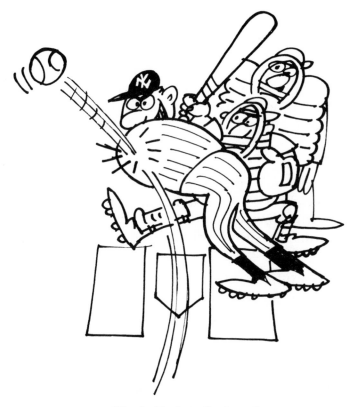

"Ouch, that strike hurt."

An Itch(y) Pitch

The Orioles have a man on first base, late in the game, as the batter works a two-oh count against the Yankee pitcher.

The runner on first, who is the potential lead run, is a good bet to steal in this situation. The Yankee manager scratches his nose. That is the sign for the pitchout.

Is it good strategy to call for a pitchout on a two-oh count?

* * *

No, it isn't good strategy to call a two-oh pitchout. If the runner does not go—which, in this case, he didn't—the pitcher, with three-oh count now, is in serious danger of walking the runner into scoring position.

* * *

Manager Billy Martin of the Yankees was guilty of this "strategy" in 1985. In a game against the Orioles, with a 2–2 tie, Baltimore had a fast runner on first. Pitcher Rich Bordi ran up a two-oh count on Lee Lacy. Martin had an itch, so he scratched his nose, probably forgetting it was a signal. The Yankees, thinking that the manager thought a play was on, called a pitchout.

The runner didn't go. Lacy proceeded to walk. And Cal Ripken followed with a game-winning hit.

You Can't Do That

The batter singles sharply to right field with a runner on second base. The team's manager, who happens to be coaching at third, waves the runner home.

But when he sees the right fielder charge the ball and fire on the run, the coach changes his mind. He cannot hold up his hands, however, because the runner is not looking at him at the time. So he reaches out and grabs the runner by the right hand and yanks the runner back to third as the outfielder throws a strike to the catcher.

Can the coach legally do this?

*   *   *

No, a coach cannot physically aid a runner in any way while the ball is a live ball. If he does, as he did here, the runner is called out. You will see the third-base coach pat a player on the rump after a home run. But that is a dead-ball situation. If the coach had done the same thing during a live-ball situation, the runner would be declared out.

*   *   *

Harold "Peanuts" Lowrey, a third-base coach for the Cubs in the 1970's, did that one day to Bobby Murcer, who was trying to score.

Throwing Behind the Runner

Trick plays can be "tricky." Take the catcher's pick-off move, for example.

A Mariner catcher was trying to contain the Royals' base runner, who was on first base. What the catcher decided to do was to look at the pitcher, as though he were throwing to the moundsman, and to throw to first base instead. The first time he attempted his trick move, his first baseman was daydreaming. The catcher's throw sailed past the unsuspecting first baseman and rolled into the right-field corner while the runner scored.

How could the catcher have prevented this unfortunate set of circumstances from taking place?

* * *

He should have informed his first baseman in advance, and he would have avoided the disastrous consequences.

* * *

Choo-Choo Coleman, catcher for the 1962 Mets, tried to hold the Dodgers' speedster Maury Wills close by using that play. Coleman actually executed the play well. The throw was hard and accurate. There was only one problem: the Mets had a first baseman by the name of Marv Throneberry.

The "Marvelous One" was daydreaming, and he caught the throw right on his forehead. The ball glanced off his head and rolled between the right and center fielders. Wills laughed all the way around the bases.

The moral is, the catcher can look the wrong way, but the first baseman can't.

"Playing first base is such fun!"

The Hasty Retreat

Oakland's center fielder is on second base ready to steal third. He gets a good jump on the Yankee pitcher as the batter flies out to the outfield. Running with his head down, the A's player doesn't see the fly being caught, and is decoyed into sliding by the Yanks' third baseman.

In doing so, he overslides third. The third-base coach, seeing what had happened, helps the runner to his feet; since the fly was caught, and the A's outfielder has to return to second, he goes directly back.

What two things are wrong with this play?

* * *

The two things wrong are 1) the third-base coach cannot physically aid the runner, and 2) the runner must retouch the base he has overslid before returning to second.

* * *

That very play occurred in a game between Oakland and New York. The A's Mike Davis overslid third, the Yankees' Graig Nettles applied the decoy, and Clete Boyer, a former Yankee third baseman, was the Oakland third-base coach.

The umpire didn't notice Boyer help Davis to his feet, but he did see that the runner failed to retouch third.

Nettles appealed the play. The umpires upheld the appeal. Davis was called out.

Double-Play Dynamite

For purposes of scoring, "1" is the pitcher; "2" the catcher; "3" the first baseman; "4" the second baseman; "5" the third baseman; "6" the shortstop; "7" the left fielder; "8" the center fielder; and "9" the right fielder.

Here's a play that seems easier to score than believe. Batting with one out and with a teammate on first base, the hitter swings and beats a ball down at his feet. He thinks that the ball is foul, but the umpire calls it fair. The catcher, trying to catch the runner at second, throws the ball past the shortstop into center field; and the center fielder proceeds to gun down the runner at third. In the meantime, the hitter remains at the plate, protesting the call. The third baseman, after applying the tag to the runner, throws the ball to the first baseman for the inning-ending double play.

If you're keeping score, what numbers do you write down in your scorebook on that play?

*   *   *

You write down the following numbers: 2–8–5–3. That's one of the most difficult plays in baseball to make. What is the lesson to be learned? Run first, argue later.

*   *   *

Len Koenecke of the 1935 Dodgers was victimized by such a play. Manager Casey Stengel, who was coaching at third base, looked on with disbelief as his outfielder hit into that bizarre double play.

In fact, Stengel was jumping up and down on his cap, urging his players to run. Instead, Koenecke was doubled at first by the greatest distance in the history of the game.

The Walking Lead

It's the last home game of the 1982 season, and Rickey Henderson of the Athletics is trying to break the record for number of stolen bases in one season.

Coming up in the ninth inning, he has a record-tying 118 thefts. He needs one to set the record. Teammate Fred Stanley is on first base with one out in a game against the visiting Tigers. Henderson tops a slow grounder down the third-base line and beats the throw to first. But Stanley stops at second.

Then Stanley, in order to create an open base for Rickey, walks off second and deliberately gets tagged out. On the next pitch, Henderson attempts to steal second, but is thrown out when the Tiger catcher calls for a pitchout. The record remains unbroken until later.

But how about Stanley? Can he deliberately make an out? Or is he subject to some form of punishment?

* * *

If the player made an out on purpose so that, as in the above example, a record could be set, the league's reaction can be harsh. Eventually, the American League's officials met and fined Stanley for allowing himself to be deliberately picked off second.

Kick Ball

The lead-off batter for the Cubs in a late-season game in Philadelphia bunts toward the right side; but as he breaks out of the batter's box, he accidentally kicks the ball up the first-base line. By the time the pitcher fields the ball and throws to the first baseman the runner has crossed the bag.

Does he get an infield hit or is he out for interference?

* * *

The runner is out when his fair ball touches him before touching a fielder.

* * *

In an Indian-A's game in Cleveland, Bert Campaneris, the lead-off batter, stepped into the batter's box as the umpire set himself up behind the plate. As the pitcher went into his windup, the umpire in the field, seeing that his partner behind the plate didn't have his mask on, called, "Time." The pitch came in, Campaneris proceeded to push a bunt towards first and to run into the rolling ball.

Ordinarily the batter would be called out; but, in this instance, the time out preceded the play. So the umpire called the offering no pitch and started the game all over again.

The Tricky Twosome

Umpires hate trick plays. With good reason. The plays usually lead to arguments. Take the following play, for example.

The manager of the Twins, let us say, likes to use a pet play when the other team has runners on first and second, two out, and a three-two count on the batter. He knows the runners will be moving; so he directs his pitcher to take his stretch and to throw to third base, instead of home.

The advance runner for the White Sox is the most surprised person in the park when he sees the third baseman waiting for him with the ball as he heads for third base.

Is this a legal play?

*   *   *

The rule book says that the pitcher cannot throw to an unoccupied base from the stretch or windup position. In this case, however, a runner was on his way and there was a play to be made at third base. Chalk one up for the Twin manager. He steals a play here.

The manager who uses this type of play will usually tip the umpire off in advance so that the arbiter isn't surprised by the play, too.

*   *   *

It has actually happened only once, and not in the majors at that. Clint Courtney, when he was a manager, liked to use this play. One night he was managing against Billy Gardner. Before the game, Courtney told the umpire that he was going to use the play, if he got the opportunity.

Late in the game, he got the opportunity. Courtney looked pleased in the dugout. There was no way, he thought, that the play could fail.

Well, there was one way: the umpire couldn't keep a secret. He had told Gardner about Courtney's plot before

"Surprised, sonny?"

the game. So when Courtney's pitcher threw to third, Gardner's runners held their places.

Remember, the pitcher can't throw to an unoccupied base, unless he is making a play. Obviously, if the runner on second is moving with the pitch, there is a play at third base. In this situation, however, the umpire took great delight in yelling, "Balk!"

The trickster was tricked.

The Hidden-Ball Trick

How important is it to keep your eyes on the ball at all times during a game? Well, consider the following hypothetical situation:

The Angels, leading the Royals in the standings by one game late in the season, get off to a 2–0 lead in their getaway contest. In the third inning the host Angels up their lead to 3–0 when their star slugger doubles a runner home.

The Royal starter storms around the mound, but finally straddles the hill to get the signal from the catcher for the next hitter. The Royal shortstop, who had taken the outfield throw, holds onto the ball. The Angel slugger, not knowing that the shortstop has the ball, steps off the bag and is promptly tagged "out" by the shortstop. The Royals have pulled the hidden-ball trick on the Angels.

Or have they?

*   *   *

No, the Royal shortstop has not legally pulled the hidden-ball trick for an out. In order for the trick play to be legal, the pitcher cannot stand on the mound. He must be standing on either the grass or the Astroturf part of the infield.

*   *   *

The hidden-ball trick led to a Cardinal victory in the 1964 World Series. After winning the first game, the Cardinals dropped two straight contests to the Yankees. When Mickey Mantle's hit opened the Yankees' lead to 3–0 in Game 4, New York seemed to have the momentum that it needed to win the Fall Classic.

But shortstop Dick Groat successfully pulled the hidden-ball trick legally on Mantle. Pitchers Roger Craig and Ron Taylor blanked the Yankees for the rest of the game.

Ken Boyer's grand-slam home run gave the Cardinals a 4–3 win and the Cardinals went on to win the Series in seven games.

Mantle's mental lapse in being picked off second base was the turning point of the Series.

That's how important it is to keep your eyes on the ball at all times during a game!

INDEX

The author practices umpiring with his sons.

About the Author

Dom Forker, the author of six books, five of which are on baseball, has studied the National Pastime closely since the age of six, when he adopted the legendary Joe DiMaggio as his diamond hero. Coincidentally, DiMaggio, playing in his first World Series, got three hits on the day that the author was born.

A player, coach, and umpire on the college, high school, sandlot, and Little League levels, Forker is fascinated by the game's uniqueness. Through experience, he has learned to expect the *unexpected*; for it usually happens.

Forker is married and has three sons, all of whom, like their father, are avid baseballl fans.